My Life, My Religion

Sikh Gurdwara

Kanwaljit Kaur-Singh
Photographs by Chris Fairclough

W
FRANKLIN WATTS
LONDON • SYDNEY

First published in 2001 by
Franklin Watts
96 Leonard Street
London EC2A 4XD

Franklin Watts Australia
56 O'Riordan Street
Alexandria
NSW 2015

ISBN 0 7496 4062 6

Dewey Decimal Classification Number 294.6

A CIP Catalogue record for this book is
available from the British Library

Series Editor: Ruth Nason
Design: Carole Binding

Reading Consultant: Lesley Clark, Reading
and Language Information Centre, University
of Reading

The Author and Publishers thank
Chatar Singh and all the people at
the Central Gurdwara, Shepherd's Bush,
for their help in preparing this book.

Printed in Malaysia

Contents

Hello!

I'm Chatar Singh. I am a Sikh and I work as a granthi at a gurdwara in London. A gurdwara is where Sikhs worship God. A granthi reads the Sikh holy book for services and ceremonies.

Our holy book is the Guru Granth Sahib. Any man, woman or child who can read it can be a granthi.

There are several volunteer granthis at our gurdwara, but volunteers do not have time to do all the duties. So I am paid to be a full-time granthi and also to look after the gurdwara building.

The Five Ks

I live with my family in a house which belongs to the gurdwara. The house is next door to the gurdwara, so I do not have far to go to work!

At 5 o'clock each morning I wash and dress to go to the gurdwara for the morning service. While I dress, I say shabads (hymns).

I make sure that I wear my kara (bracelet), kach (shorts) and kirpan (sword). I comb my kes (un-cut hair) with a kanga (comb) and cover it with my turban. These five things beginning with a K show that I am a Sikh.

The Guru Granth Sahib

The Guru Granth Sahib tells us what the Sikh Gurus taught about God and about the right way to live.

We treat it with great respect. It is covered with beautiful cloths. At night it is kept safe in a small room in the gurdwara. Every morning I carry it out into the prayer hall.

I place the Guru Granth Sahib on pillows, on a platform under a canopy. Then I cover it again with beautiful cloths. It stays there for the whole day for people to read.

The day's message

Every day I lead two services in the gurdwara – one in the morning and one in the evening.

At each service I lift some pages of the Guru Granth Sahib and let them fall open. Then I read aloud from the page, in Punjabi. The reading is called the vak – the message for the day.

The Guru Granth Sahib begins with the words of Guru Nanak. He started Sikhism in India 500 years ago.

Guru Nanak and the other Sikh Gurus taught that there is only one God. God made all people and loves them equally. The Sikh symbol called the Ik Onkar means 'one God'.

Preparing langar

Everyone is welcome at our services and we all eat together afterwards. The meal that we eat is called langar and the room where we eat it is also called the langar.

Many people come to the service on Sunday evenings. So, on Sundays, I shop and then help to cook langar.

We always cook vegetarian food so that everyone can eat it.

Men, women and children all help to prepare langar. We start cooking at 12 noon and finish by 5.30. Then I go home to get ready for the evening service.

The evening service

The service starts at 6.30. People always take off their shoes and cover their head before they enter the prayer hall. In the prayer hall they bow in front of the Guru Granth Sahib and then sit down.

I sit behind the Guru Granth Sahib and wave a chaur over it. The chaur is like a fan. All these actions show respect for the Gurus' teachings.

During the service the ragis (musicians) or other people sing shabads (hymns) from the Guru Granth Sahib.

My son and I also sing together. He plays the tabla (drums) and I play the harmonium.

After the singing, I say the ardas (the main prayer).

Then I open the Guru Granth Sahib and read the vak.

After the service

At the end of the service, one of the people there gives out a sweet called krah prashad. This reminds us that sharing is very important.

Then everyone goes into the langar. We eat together to show that we are all members of God's family.

Special events

Sikhs have a naming ceremony for a new baby. I open the Guru Granth Sahib and read a shabad (hymn). Then the baby's family chooses a name beginning with the first letter of the shabad. This baby was named Baljit Singh. Singh is the second name of all Sikh boys. The second name of all Sikh girls is Kaur.

Sikhs never cut their hair. So, to keep their long hair tidy, boys wear a patka and men wear a turban. Many boys have their first turban tied at a special service in the gurdwara.

At a Sikh wedding, the couple walk around the Guru Granth Sahib four times. This is to show that they will follow the Gurus' teachings all through their lives.

A busy day

It's a busy life being a granthi and looking after the gurdwara.

Many people come to arrange a date for their turn to cook langar.

The gurdwara is being painted and I have to check that it is being done correctly.

During services in the gurdwara I am sitting for many hours. So I like to do keep-fit exercises at home each day.

In the afternoons children come to the gurdwara to learn Punjabi. It is important for Sikh children to learn this language so that they can read and understand the teachings of our Gurus in the Guru Granth Sahib.

I also meet with the people who run the gurdwara. For example, we plan the celebrations for the festival of Guru Nanak's Birthday.

To end the day, I enjoy having a quiet time to study the Sikh scriptures.

Glossary

ardas

The main Sikh prayer. In this prayer Sikhs remember God and the Sikh Gurus. Then they ask God to care for all people.

ceremony

Something we do on special occasions, usually in the same way every time.

Five Ks

A kind of uniform that Guru Gobind Singh told Sikhs to wear.

Guru Granth Sahib

The Sikh holy book. It is written in Punjabi.

kach

White undershorts, one of the Five Ks. They are a sign of purity.

kanga

A wooden comb, one of the Five Ks. It is a sign of cleanliness.

kara

A steel bracelet, one of the Five Ks. The steel is a sign of strength. The round shape reminds Sikhs that God has no beginning and no end.

Kaur

A name that Guru Gobind Singh, the tenth Sikh Guru, gave to all Sikh females. It means 'princess'.

kes

Un-cut hair. Sikhs never cut their hair. This follows the example of the Sikh Gurus.

kirpan

A small sword, one of the Five Ks. It is a sign that Sikhs are ready to defend the weak.

krah prashad

A sweet made of equal amounts of semolina, butter, sugar and water. It is shared after services, to show that everyone is equal.

patka

A head covering worn by Sikh boys over their tied-up long hair.

Punjabi

The language spoken in the Punjab, the area of northern India where Sikhism started.

service

A meeting to pray to God.

Sikh Gurus

The ten leaders and teachers of the Sikhs in the first 200 years of the religion. The first Guru was Guru Nanak. The last Guru was Guru Gobind Singh. He told Sikhs always to follow the teachings in the Guru Granth Sahib.

Singh

A name that Guru Gobind Singh, the tenth Sikh Guru, gave to all Sikh males. It means 'lion'.

turban

A long piece of cloth that a Sikh man winds around his head to keep his hair (kes) tidy.

volunteer

Someone who does a job without being paid for it.

Index